2022
BUDGET PLANNER

NAME:
_____

PHONE:
_____

EMAIL:
_____

HOW TO USE THIS FINANCIAL PLANNER:

One of the biggest pitfalls in financial planning is overcomplication and not following through. Therefore, the design of this planner has been intentionally kept simple and easy to use. You can fill out the sections that apply to you and skip the ones that you don't need at the moment. It has also been kept free of any pre-filled areas that you may not require in your current situation.

The **FINANCIAL SUMMARY** section has been organized for quick access to your current account information and your financial status. In this section you will be able to:

- gather all the accounts you have open with your financial institutions, bill companies, and/or creditors (including any outstanding loans from family or friends).

- monitor your major savings goals with several detailed savings trackers with areas to input your goals, deadlines, deposits and/or withdrawls.

- keep track of your debt repayments with a quick overview of how you are progressing throughout the year and where your balance stands at any given month. (*You can keep coming back to this section at the end of every month to keep it up to date*).

- keep track of your fixed or variable bill payments throughout the year to make sure you haven't missed any months.

- view your overall financial situation including your current assets (cash, investments, real estate, etc), liabilities (debts, loans, mortgage, etc.), credit score and net worth.

The **MONTHLY PLANNER** section has been designed to provide you with a more detailed look at how you manage your money every month. This includes your income sources, savings, fixed and variable expenses, a more detailed debt/loan repayment breakdown, and simple spending trackers to monitor your small day to day purchases.

A quick summary where you feel improvements can be made has also been included on the notes pages provided at the end of each month.

Wherever your are on your financial journey, I hope this simple budget planner will make your life easier by helping you keep track of where your money is going every month and providing you with the opportunity to make wise financial decisions everyday.

Happy Planning!

Emmeline Bloom

Questions or Customer Service?

Email me at:
hello@emmelinebloom.com

[I AM ON THE ROAD TO FINANCIAL FREEDOM]

YEAR AHEAD

2022 | JANUARY

S	M	T	W	T	F	S
						1
2	3	4	5	6	7	8
9	10	11	12	13	14	15
16	17	18	19	20	21	22
23	24	25	26	27	28	29
30	31					

2022 | FEBRUARY

S	M	T	W	T	F	S
		1	2	3	4	5
6	7	8	9	10	11	12
13	14	15	16	17	18	19
20	21	22	23	24	25	26
27	28					

2022 | MARCH

S	M	T	W	T	F	S
		1	2	3	4	5
6	7	8	9	10	11	12
13	14	15	16	17	18	19
20	21	22	23	24	25	26
27	28	29	30	31		

2022 | APRIL

S	M	T	W	T	F	S
					1	2
3	4	5	6	7	8	9
10	11	12	13	14	15	16
17	18	19	20	21	22	23
24	25	26	27	28	29	30

2022 | MAY

S	M	T	W	T	F	S
1	2	3	4	5	6	7
8	9	10	11	12	13	14
15	16	17	18	19	20	21
22	23	24	25	26	27	28
29	30	31				

2022 | JUNE

S	M	T	W	T	F	S
			1	2	3	4
5	6	7	8	9	10	11
12	13	14	15	16	17	18
19	20	21	22	23	24	25
26	27	28	29	30		

2022 | JULY

S	M	T	W	T	F	S
					1	2
3	4	5	6	7	8	9
10	11	12	13	14	15	16
17	18	19	20	21	22	23
24	25	26	27	28	29	30
31						

2022 | AUGUST

S	M	T	W	T	F	S
	1	2	3	4	5	6
7	8	9	10	11	12	13
14	15	16	17	18	19	20
21	22	23	24	25	26	27
28	29	30	31			

2022 | SEPTEMBER

S	M	T	W	T	F	S
				1	2	3
4	5	6	7	8	9	10
11	12	13	14	15	16	17
18	19	20	21	22	23	24
25	26	27	28	29	30	

2022 | OCTOBER

S	M	T	W	T	F	S
						1
2	3	4	5	6	7	8
9	10	11	12	13	14	15
16	17	18	19	20	21	22
23	24	25	26	27	28	29
30	31					

2022 | NOVEMBER

S	M	T	W	T	F	S
		1	2	3	4	5
6	7	8	9	10	11	12
13	14	15	16	17	18	19
20	21	22	23	24	25	26
27	28	29	30			

2022 | DECEMBER

S	M	T	W	T	F	S
				1	2	3
4	5	6	7	8	9	10
11	12	13	14	15	16	17
18	19	20	21	22	23	24
25	26	27	28	29	30	31

NOTES

FINANCIAL GOALS

THIS YEAR MY PRIMARY GOALS ARE:

JAN MY GOALS THIS MONTH

FEB MY GOALS THIS MONTH

MAR MY GOALS THIS MONTH

APR MY GOALS THIS MONTH

MAY MY GOALS THIS MONTH

JUN MY GOALS THIS MONTH

JUL MY GOALS THIS MONTH

AUG MY GOALS THIS MONTH

SEP MY GOALS THIS MONTH

OCT MY GOALS THIS MONTH

NOV MY GOALS THIS MONTH

DEC MY GOALS THIS MONTH

BANK ACCOUNTS

ACCOUNT #1

FINANCIAL INSTITUTION		ACCOUNT #
NAME ON ACCOUNT		ACCOUNT TYPE
CARD #	PIN #	ROUTING/TRANSIT #
WEBSITE URL	USERNAME	PASSWORD
NOTES		

ACCOUNT #2

FINANCIAL INSTITUTION		ACCOUNT #
NAME ON ACCOUNT		ACCOUNT TYPE
CARD #	PIN #	ROUTING/TRANSIT #
WEBSITE URL	USERNAME	PASSWORD
NOTES		

ACCOUNT #3

FINANCIAL INSTITUTION		ACCOUNT #
NAME ON ACCOUNT		ACCOUNT TYPE
CARD #	PIN #	ROUTING/TRANSIT #
WEBSITE URL	USERNAME	PASSWORD
NOTES		

ACCOUNT #4

FINANCIAL INSTITUTION		ACCOUNT #
NAME ON ACCOUNT		ACCOUNT TYPE
CARD #	PIN #	ROUTING/TRANSIT #
WEBSITE URL	USERNAME	PASSWORD
NOTES		

BANK ACCOUNTS

ACCOUNT #5

FINANCIAL INSTITUTION		ACCOUNT #
NAME ON ACCOUNT		ACCOUNT TYPE
CARD #	PIN #	ROUTING/TRANSIT #
WEBSITE URL	USERNAME	PASSWORD
NOTES		

ACCOUNT #6

FINANCIAL INSTITUTION		ACCOUNT #
NAME ON ACCOUNT		ACCOUNT TYPE
CARD #	PIN #	ROUTING/TRANSIT #
WEBSITE URL	USERNAME	PASSWORD
NOTES		

ACCOUNT #7

FINANCIAL INSTITUTION		ACCOUNT #
NAME ON ACCOUNT		ACCOUNT TYPE
CARD #	PIN #	ROUTING/TRANSIT #
WEBSITE URL	USERNAME	PASSWORD
NOTES		

ACCOUNT #8

FINANCIAL INSTITUTION		ACCOUNT #
NAME ON ACCOUNT		ACCOUNT TYPE
CARD #	PIN #	ROUTING/TRANSIT #
WEBSITE URL	USERNAME	PASSWORD
NOTES		

DEBT ACCOUNTS

DEBT ACCOUNT #1

COMPANY		ACCOUNT #
NAME ON ACCOUNT		CREDIT TYPE
CARD #	PIN #	CREDIT LIMIT
WEBSITE URL	USERNAME	PASSWORD
NOTES		CURRENT BALANCE

DEBT ACCOUNT #2

COMPANY		ACCOUNT #
NAME ON ACCOUNT		CREDIT TYPE
CARD #	PIN #	CREDIT LIMIT
WEBSITE URL	USERNAME	PASSWORD
NOTES		CURRENT BALANCE

DEBT ACCOUNT #3

COMPANY		ACCOUNT #
NAME ON ACCOUNT		CREDIT TYPE
CARD #	PIN #	CREDIT LIMIT
WEBSITE URL	USERNAME	PASSWORD
NOTES		CURRENT BALANCE

DEBT ACCOUNT #4

COMPANY		ACCOUNT #
NAME ON ACCOUNT		CREDIT TYPE
CARD #	PIN #	CREDIT LIMIT
WEBSITE URL	USERNAME	PASSWORD
NOTES		CURRENT BALANCE

DEBT ACCOUNTS

DEBT ACCOUNT #5

COMPANY		ACCOUNT #
NAME ON ACCOUNT		CREDIT TYPE
CARD #	PIN #	CREDIT LIMIT
WEBSITE URL	USERNAME	PASSWORD
NOTES		CURRENT BALANCE

DEBT ACCOUNT #6

COMPANY		ACCOUNT #
NAME ON ACCOUNT		CREDIT TYPE
CARD #	PIN #	CREDIT LIMIT
WEBSITE URL	USERNAME	PASSWORD
NOTES		CURRENT BALANCE

DBET ACCOUNT #7

COMPANY		ACCOUNT #
NAME ON ACCOUNT		CREDIT TYPE
CARD #	PIN #	CREDIT LIMIT
WEBSITE URL	USERNAME	PASSWORD
NOTES		CURRENT BALANCE

DEBT ACCOUNT #8

COMPANY		ACCOUNT #
NAME ON ACCOUNT		CREDIT TYPE
CARD #	PIN #	CREDIT LIMIT
WEBSITE URL	USERNAME	PASSWORD
NOTES		CURRENT BALANCE

BILL ACCOUNTS

COMPANY	ACCOUNT #	
NAME ON ACCOUNT	PHONE #	
WEBSITE URL	USERNAME	PASSWORD
NOTES		

COMPANY	ACCOUNT #	
NAME ON ACCOUNT	PHONE #	
WEBSITE URL	USERNAME	PASSWORD
NOTES		

COMPANY	ACCOUNT #	
NAME ON ACCOUNT	PHONE #	
WEBSITE URL	USERNAME	PASSWORD
NOTES		

COMPANY	ACCOUNT #	
NAME ON ACCOUNT	PHONE #	
WEBSITE URL	USERNAME	PASSWORD
NOTES		

COMPANY	ACCOUNT #	
NAME ON ACCOUNT	PHONE #	
WEBSITE URL	USERNAME	PASSWORD
NOTES		

BILL ACCOUNTS

COMPANY	ACCOUNT #	
NAME ON ACCOUNT	PHONE #	
WEBSITE URL	USERNAME	PASSWORD
NOTES		

COMPANY	ACCOUNT #	
NAME ON ACCOUNT	PHONE #	
WEBSITE URL	USERNAME	PASSWORD
NOTES		

COMPANY	ACCOUNT #	
NAME ON ACCOUNT	PHONE #	
WEBSITE URL	USERNAME	PASSWORD
NOTES		

COMPANY	ACCOUNT #	
NAME ON ACCOUNT	PHONE #	
WEBSITE URL	USERNAME	PASSWORD
NOTES		

COMPANY	ACCOUNT #	
NAME ON ACCOUNT	PHONE #	
WEBSITE URL	USERNAME	PASSWORD
NOTES		

BILL ACCOUNTS

COMPANY	ACCOUNT #	
NAME ON ACCOUNT	PHONE #	
WEBSITE URL	USERNAME	PASSWORD
NOTES		

COMPANY	ACCOUNT #	
NAME ON ACCOUNT	PHONE #	
WEBSITE URL	USERNAME	PASSWORD
NOTES		

COMPANY	ACCOUNT #	
NAME ON ACCOUNT	PHONE #	
WEBSITE URL	USERNAME	PASSWORD
NOTES		

COMPANY	ACCOUNT #	
NAME ON ACCOUNT	PHONE #	
WEBSITE URL	USERNAME	PASSWORD
NOTES		

COMPANY	ACCOUNT #	
NAME ON ACCOUNT	PHONE #	
WEBSITE URL	USERNAME	PASSWORD
NOTES		

BILL ACCOUNTS

COMPANY	ACCOUNT #	
NAME ON ACCOUNT	PHONE #	
WEBSITE URL	USERNAME	PASSWORD
NOTES		

COMPANY	ACCOUNT #	
NAME ON ACCOUNT	PHONE #	
WEBSITE URL	USERNAME	PASSWORD
NOTES		

COMPANY	ACCOUNT #	
NAME ON ACCOUNT	PHONE #	
WEBSITE URL	USERNAME	PASSWORD
NOTES		

COMPANY	ACCOUNT #	
NAME ON ACCOUNT	PHONE #	
WEBSITE URL	USERNAME	PASSWORD
NOTES		

COMPANY	ACCOUNT #	
NAME ON ACCOUNT	PHONE #	
WEBSITE URL	USERNAME	PASSWORD
NOTES		

SAVINGS TRACKER

SAVING FOR		
STARTING BALANCE		
SAVINGS GOAL		
DEADLINE		
COMMENTS		

DATE	AMOUNT	TOTAL

SAVING FOR		
STARTING BALANCE		
SAVINGS GOAL		
DEADLINE		
COMMENTS		

DATE	AMOUNT	TOTAL

SAVINGS TRACKER

SAVING FOR		
STARTING BALANCE		
SAVINGS GOAL		
DEADLINE		
COMMENTS		

DATE	AMOUNT	TOTAL

SAVING FOR		
STARTING BALANCE		
SAVINGS GOAL		
DEADLINE		
COMMENTS		

DATE	AMOUNT	TOTAL

SAVINGS TRACKER

SAVING FOR

STARTING BALANCE

SAVINGS GOAL

DEADLINE

COMMENTS

DATE	AMOUNT	TOTAL

SAVING FOR

STARTING BALANCE

SAVINGS GOAL

DEADLINE

COMMENTS

DATE	AMOUNT	TOTAL

SAVINGS TRACKER

SAVING FOR	
STARTING BALANCE	
SAVINGS GOAL	
DEADLINE	
COMMENTS	

DATE	AMOUNT	TOTAL

SAVING FOR	
STARTING BALANCE	
SAVINGS GOAL	
DEADLINE	
COMMENTS	

DATE	AMOUNT	TOTAL

DEBT PAYMENT TRACKER

CREDITORS									
STARTING BALANCE									
JANUARY	PAYMENT								
	BALANCE								
FEBRUARY	PAYMENT								
	BALANCE								
MARCH	PAYMENT								
	BALANCE								
APRIL	PAYMENT								
	BALANCE								
MAY	PAYMENT								
	BALANCE								
JUNE	PAYMENT								
	BALANCE								
JULY	PAYMENT								
	BALANCE								
AUGUST	PAYMENT								
	BALANCE								
SEPTEMBER	PAYMENT								
	BALANCE								
OCTOBER	PAYMENT								
	BALANCE								
NOVEMBER	PAYMENT								
	BALANCE								
DECEMBER	PAYMENT								
	BALANCE								

BILL PAYMENT TRACKER

#	ACCOUNT	DUE	JAN ☑	FEB ☑	MAR ☑	APR ☑	MAY ☑	JUN ☑	JUL ☑	AUG ☑	SEP ☑	OCT ☑	NOV ☑	DEC ☑
1														
2														
3														
4														
5														
6														
7														
8														
9														
10														
11														
12														
13														
14														
15														
16														
17														
18														
19														
20														

NOTES

_____

_____

_____

_____

CHECK REGISTER

#	CODE/ NUMBER	DATE	DESCRIPTION	PAYMENT DEBIT (–)		PAYMENT CREDIT (+)		BALANCE	
1									
2									
3									
4									
5									
6									
7									
8									
9									
10									
11									
12									
13									
14									
15									
16									
17									
18									
19									
20									
21									
22									
23									
24									
25									

CHECK REGISTER

#	CODE/ NUMBER	DATE	DESCRIPTION	PAYMENT DEBIT (-)	PAYMENT CREDIT (+)	BALANCE	
26							
27							
28							
29							
30							
31							
32							
33							
34							
35							
36							
37							
38							
39							
40							
41							
42							
43							
44							
45							
46							
47							
48							
49							
50							

FINANCIAL SUMMARY

DATE	
CREDIT SCORE	
NET WORTH	

FINANCIALS	
ASSETS TOTAL	LIABILITIES TOTAL

	ASSETS	AMOUNT
CASH		
	SUBTOTAL	
INVESTMENTS		
	SUBTOTAL	
	SUBTOTAL	
	SUBTOTAL	

	LIABILITIES	AMOUNT
DEBTS		
	SUBTOTAL	
LOANS		
	SUBTOTAL	
	SUBTOTAL	
	SUBTOTAL	

It's not your salary that makes you rich, it's your spending habits.

- Charles A. Jaffe

JANUARY

NOTES	SUNDAY	MONDAY	TUESDAY
	2	3	4
	9	10	11
	16	17	18
	23	24	25
	30	31	

GOALS

OVERVIEW

WEDNESDAY	THURSDAY	FRIDAY	SATURDAY
			1
5	6	7	8
12	13	14	15
19	20	21	22
26	27	28	29

*A budget is telling your money where to go
instead of wondering where it went.*

- Dave Ramsey

MONTHLY BUDGET

INCOME

DATE	SOURCE	AMOUNT
	TOTAL	

SAVINGS

BUDGETED	ACTUAL
DIFFERENCE	

FIXED EXPENSES

#	DESCRIPTION	DUE DATE	AMOUNT	PAID	COMMENT
1				○	
2				○	
3				○	
4				○	
5				○	
6				○	
7				○	
8				○	
9				○	
10				○	
11				○	
12				○	
13				○	
14				○	
15				○	
16				○	
17				○	
18				○	
19				○	
20				○	

MONTHLY BUDGET

VARIABLE EXPENSES

#	DESCRIPTION	DATE	AMOUNT	PAID	COMMENT
21				○	
22				○	
23				○	
24				○	
25				○	
26				○	
27				○	
28				○	
29				○	
30				○	
31				○	
32				○	
33				○	
34				○	
35				○	
36				○	
37				○	
38				○	
39				○	
40				○	
41				○	
42				○	

MONTHLY SUMMARY

	BUDGETED	ACTUAL	DIFFERENCE
TOTAL INCOME			
TOTAL FIXED EXPENSES			
TOTAL VARIABLE EXPENSES			

DEBT REPAYMENT

DATE	ACCOUNT	STARTING BALANCE	MINIMUM PAYMENT	ADDITIONAL PAYMENT	BALANCE
TOTAL SPENT ON DEBTS THIS MONTH					

DAILY SPENDING TRACKER

JANUARY 01	SPENT	JANUARY 05	SPENT

JANUARY 02	SPENT	JANUARY 06	SPENT

JANUARY 03	SPENT	JANUARY 07	SPENT

JANUARY 04	SPENT	JANUARY 08	SPENT

DAILY SPENDING TRACKER

JANUARY 09	SPENT	JANUARY 13	SPENT

JANUARY 10	SPENT	JANUARY 14	SPENT

JANUARY 11	SPENT	JANUARY 15	SPENT

JANUARY 12	SPENT	JANUARY 16	SPENT

DAILY SPENDING TRACKER

JANUARY 17	SPENT	JANUARY 21	SPENT

JANUARY 18	SPENT	JANUARY 22	SPENT

JANUARY 19	SPENT	JANUARY 23	SPENT

JANUARY 20	SPENT	JANUARY 24	SPENT

DAILY SPENDING TRACKER

JANUARY 25	SPENT	JANUARY 29	SPENT

JANUARY 26	SPENT	JANUARY 30	SPENT

JANUARY 27	SPENT	JANUARY 31	SPENT

JANUARY 28	SPENT		
		TOTAL DAILY SPEND THIS MONTH	

NOTES

_____
_____
_____
_____
_____
_____
_____
_____
_____
_____
_____
_____
_____
_____
_____
_____
_____
_____
_____
_____
_____
_____
_____
_____
_____

WHERE DID I HAVE THE MOST DIFFICULTY	HOW CAN I IMPROVE NEXT MONTH

FEBRUARY

NOTES	SUNDAY	MONDAY	TUESDAY
			1
	6	7	8
	13	14	15
	20	21	22
	27	28	

GOALS

OVERVIEW

WEDNESDAY	THURSDAY	FRIDAY	SATURDAY
2	3	4	5
9	10	11	12
16	17	18	19
23	24	25	26

A goal without a plan is just a wish.

- Antoine de Saint-Exupery

MONTHLY BUDGET

INCOME

DATE	SOURCE	AMOUNT
	TOTAL	

SAVINGS

BUDGETED	ACTUAL
DIFFERENCE	

FIXED EXPENSES

#	DESCRIPTION	DUE DATE	AMOUNT	PAID	COMMENT
1				○	
2				○	
3				○	
4				○	
5				○	
6				○	
7				○	
8				○	
9				○	
10				○	
11				○	
12				○	
13				○	
14				○	
15				○	
16				○	
17				○	
18				○	
19				○	
20				○	

MONTHLY BUDGET

VARIABLE EXPENSES

#	DESCRIPTION	DATE	AMOUNT	PAID	COMMENT
21				○	
22				○	
23				○	
24				○	
25				○	
26				○	
27				○	
28				○	
29				○	
30				○	
31				○	
32				○	
33				○	
34				○	
35				○	
36				○	
37				○	
38				○	
39				○	
40				○	
41				○	
42				○	

MONTHLY SUMMARY

	BUDGETED	ACTUAL	DIFFERENCE
TOTAL INCOME			
TOTAL FIXED EXPENSES			
TOTAL VARIABLE EXPENSES			

DEBT REPAYMENT

DATE	ACCOUNT	STARTING BALANCE	MINIMUM PAYMENT	ADDITIONAL PAYMENT	BALANCE
TOTAL SPENT ON DEBTS THIS MONTH					

DAILY SPENDING TRACKER

FEBRUARY 01	SPENT	FEBRUARY 05	SPENT

FEBRUARY 02	SPENT	FEBRUARY 06	SPENT

FEBRUARY 03	SPENT	FEBRUARY 07	SPENT

FEBRUARY 04	SPENT	FEBRUARY 08	SPENT

DAILY SPENDING TRACKER

FEBRUARY 09	SPENT	FEBRUARY 13	SPENT

FEBRUARY 10	SPENT	FEBRUARY 14	SPENT

FEBRUARY 11	SPENT	FEBRUARY 15	SPENT

FEBRUARY 12	SPENT	FEBRUARY 16	SPENT

DAILY SPENDING TRACKER

FEBRUARY 17	SPENT	FEBRUARY 21	SPENT

FEBRUARY 18	SPENT	FEBRUARY 22	SPENT

FEBRUARY 19	SPENT	FEBRUARY 23	SPENT

FEBRUARY 20	SPENT	FEBRUARY 24	SPENT

DAILY SPENDING TRACKER

FEBRUARY 25	SPENT		

FEBRUARY 26	SPENT		

FEBRUARY 27	SPENT		

FEBRUARY 28	SPENT		
		TOTAL DAILY SPEND THIS MONTH	

NOTES

_____
_____
_____
_____
_____
_____
_____
_____
_____
_____
_____
_____
_____
_____
_____
_____
_____
_____
_____
_____
_____
_____
_____
_____
_____

WHERE DID I HAVE THE MOST DIFFICULTY	HOW CAN I IMPROVE NEXT MONTH

MARCH

NOTES	SUNDAY	MONDAY	TUESDAY
			1
	6	7	8
	13	14	15
	20	21	22
	27	28	29

GOALS

OVERVIEW

WEDNESDAY	THURSDAY	FRIDAY	SATURDAY
2	3	4	5
9	10	11	12
16	17	18	19
23	24	25	26
30	31		

AFFIRMATION:

I am capable of creating my dream life.

MONTHLY BUDGET

INCOME

DATE	SOURCE	AMOUNT
	TOTAL	

SAVINGS

BUDGETED	ACTUAL
DIFFERENCE	

FIXED EXPENSES

#	DESCRIPTION	DUE DATE	AMOUNT	PAID	COMMENT
1				◯	
2				◯	
3				◯	
4				◯	
5				◯	
6				◯	
7				◯	
8				◯	
9				◯	
10				◯	
11				◯	
12				◯	
13				◯	
14				◯	
15				◯	
16				◯	
17				◯	
18				◯	
19				◯	
20				◯	

MONTHLY BUDGET

VARIABLE EXPENSES

#	DESCRIPTION	DATE	AMOUNT	PAID	COMMENT
21				○	
22				○	
23				○	
24				○	
25				○	
26				○	
27				○	
28				○	
29				○	
30				○	
31				○	
32				○	
33				○	
34				○	
35				○	
36				○	
37				○	
38				○	
39				○	
40				○	
41				○	
42				○	

MONTHLY SUMMARY

	BUDGETED	ACTUAL	DIFFERENCE
TOTAL INCOME			
TOTAL FIXED EXPENSES			
TOTAL VARIABLE EXPENSES			

DEBT REPAYMENT

DATE	ACCOUNT	STARTING BALANCE	MINIMUM PAYMENT	ADDITIONAL PAYMENT	BALANCE
TOTAL SPENT ON DEBTS THIS MONTH					

DAILY SPENDING TRACKER

MARCH 01	SPENT	MARCH 05	SPENT

MARCH 02	SPENT	MARCH 06	SPENT

MARCH 03	SPENT	MARCH 07	SPENT

MARCH 04	SPENT	MARCH 08	SPENT

DAILY SPENDING TRACKER

MARCH 09	SPENT	MARCH 13	SPENT

MARCH 10	SPENT	MARCH 14	SPENT

MARCH 11	SPENT	MARCH 15	SPENT

MARCH 12	SPENT	MARCH 16	SPENT

DAILY SPENDING TRACKER

MARCH 17	SPENT	MARCH 21	SPENT

MARCH 18	SPENT	MARCH 22	SPENT

MARCH 19	SPENT	MARCH 23	SPENT

MARCH 20	SPENT	MARCH 24	SPENT

DAILY SPENDING TRACKER

MARCH 25	SPENT	MARCH 29	SPENT

MARCH 26	SPENT	MARCH 30	SPENT

MARCH 27	SPENT	MARCH 31	SPENT

MARCH 28	SPENT		
		TOTAL DAILY SPEND THIS MONTH	

NOTES

_____
_____
_____
_____
_____
_____
_____
_____
_____
_____
_____
_____
_____
_____
_____
_____
_____
_____
_____
_____
_____
_____
_____
_____
_____
_____

WHERE DID I HAVE THE MOST DIFFICULTY	HOW CAN I IMPROVE NEXT MONTH

APRIL

NOTES	SUNDAY	MONDAY	TUESDAY
	3	4	5
	10	11	12
	17	18	19
	24	25	26

GOALS

OVERVIEW

WEDNESDAY	THURSDAY	FRIDAY	SATURDAY
		1	2
6	7	8	9
13	14	15	16
20	21	22	23
27	28	29	30

Learn to save first and spend afterwards.

- John Poole

MONTHLY BUDGET

INCOME

DATE	SOURCE	AMOUNT
	TOTAL	

SAVINGS

BUDGETED	ACTUAL
DIFFERENCE	

FIXED EXPENSES

#	DESCRIPTION	DUE DATE	AMOUNT	PAID	COMMENT
1				○	
2				○	
3				○	
4				○	
5				○	
6				○	
7				○	
8				○	
9				○	
10				○	
11				○	
12				○	
13				○	
14				○	
15				○	
16				○	
17				○	
18				○	
19				○	
20				○	

MONTHLY BUDGET

VARIABLE EXPENSES

#	DESCRIPTION	DATE	AMOUNT	PAID	COMMENT
21				○	
22				○	
23				○	
24				○	
25				○	
26				○	
27				○	
28				○	
29				○	
30				○	
31				○	
32				○	
33				○	
34				○	
35				○	
36				○	
37				○	
38				○	
39				○	
40				○	
41				○	
42				○	

MONTHLY SUMMARY

	BUDGETED	ACTUAL	DIFFERENCE
TOTAL INCOME			
TOTAL FIXED EXPENSES			
TOTAL VARIABLE EXPENSES			

DEBT REPAYMENT

DATE	ACCOUNT	STARTING BALANCE	MINIMUM PAYMENT	ADDITIONAL PAYMENT	BALANCE
TOTAL SPENT ON DEBTS THIS MONTH					

DAILY SPENDING TRACKER

APRIL 01	SPENT	APRIL 05	SPENT

APRIL 02	SPENT	APRIL 06	SPENT

APRIL 03	SPENT	APRIL 07	SPENT

APRIL 04	SPENT	APRIL 08	SPENT

DAILY SPENDING TRACKER

APRIL 09	SPENT	APRIL 13	SPENT

APRIL 10	SPENT	APRIL 14	SPENT

APRIL 11	SPENT	APRIL 15	SPENT

APRIL 12	SPENT	APRIL 16	SPENT

DAILY SPENDING TRACKER

APRIL 17	SPENT	APRIL 21	SPENT

APRIL 18	SPENT	APRIL 22	SPENT

APRIL 19	SPENT	APRIL 23	SPENT

APRIL 20	SPENT	APRIL 24	SPENT

DAILY SPENDING TRACKER

APRIL 25	SPENT	APRIL 29	SPENT

APRIL 26	SPENT	APRIL 30	SPENT

APRIL 27	SPENT

APRIL 28	SPENT

TOTAL DAILY SPEND THIS MONTH

NOTES

WHERE DID I HAVE THE MOST DIFFICULTY

HOW CAN I IMPROVE NEXT MONTH

MAY

NOTES	SUNDAY	MONDAY	TUESDAY
	1	2	3
	8	9	10
	15	16	17
	22	23	24
	29	30	31

GOALS

OVERVIEW

WEDNESDAY	THURSDAY	FRIDAY	SATURDAY
4	5	6	7
11	12	13	14
18	19	20	21
25	26	27	28

AFFIRMATION:

I welcome abundance into my life daily.

MONTHLY BUDGET

INCOME

DATE	SOURCE	AMOUNT
	TOTAL	

SAVINGS

BUDGETED	ACTUAL
DIFFERENCE	

FIXED EXPENSES

#	DESCRIPTION	DUE DATE	AMOUNT	PAID	COMMENT
1				○	
2				○	
3				○	
4				○	
5				○	
6				○	
7				○	
8				○	
9				○	
10				○	
11				○	
12				○	
13				○	
14				○	
15				○	
16				○	
17				○	
18				○	
19				○	
20				○	

MONTHLY BUDGET

VARIABLE EXPENSES

#	DESCRIPTION	DATE	AMOUNT	PAID	COMMENT
21				○	
22				○	
23				○	
24				○	
25				○	
26				○	
27				○	
28				○	
29				○	
30				○	
31				○	
32				○	
33				○	
34				○	
35				○	
36				○	
37				○	
38				○	
39				○	
40				○	
41				○	
42				○	

MONTHLY SUMMARY

	BUDGETED	ACTUAL	DIFFERENCE
TOTAL INCOME			
TOTAL FIXED EXPENSES			
TOTAL VARIABLE EXPENSES			

DEBT REPAYMENT

DATE	ACCOUNT	STARTING BALANCE	MINIMUM PAYMENT	ADDITIONAL PAYMENT	BALANCE
		TOTAL SPENT ON DEBTS THIS MONTH			

DAILY SPENDING TRACKER

MAY 01	SPENT	MAY 05	SPENT

MAY 02	SPENT	MAY 06	SPENT

MAY 03	SPENT	MAY 07	SPENT

MAY 04	SPENT	MAY 08	SPENT

DAILY SPENDING TRACKER

MAY 09	SPENT	MAY 13	SPENT

MAY 10	SPENT	MAY 14	SPENT

MAY 11	SPENT	MAY 15	SPENT

MAY 12	SPENT	MAY 16	SPENT

DAILY SPENDING TRACKER

MAY 17	SPENT	MAY 21	SPENT

MAY 18	SPENT	MAY 22	SPENT

MAY 19	SPENT	MAY 23	SPENT

MAY 20	SPENT	MAY 24	SPENT

DAILY SPENDING TRACKER

MAY 25	SPENT	MAY 29	SPENT

MAY 26	SPENT	MAY 30	SPENT

MAY 27	SPENT	MAY 31	SPENT

MAY 28	SPENT		

TOTAL DAILY SPEND THIS MONTH	

NOTES

WHERE DID I HAVE THE MOST DIFFICULTY	HOW CAN I IMPROVE NEXT MONTH

JUNE

NOTES	SUNDAY	MONDAY	TUESDAY
_____ _____			
	5	6	7
	12	13	14
	19	20	21
	26	27	28

GOALS

_____

_____

_____

_____

OVERVIEW

WEDNESDAY	THURSDAY	FRIDAY	SATURDAY
1	2	3	4
8	9	10	11
15	16	17	18
22	23	24	25
29	30		

Be happy with what you have, while working for what you want.

- Helen Keller

MONTHLY BUDGET

INCOME

DATE	SOURCE	AMOUNT
	TOTAL	

SAVINGS

BUDGETED	ACTUAL
DIFFERENCE	

FIXED EXPENSES

#	DESCRIPTION	DUE DATE	AMOUNT	PAID	COMMENT
1				○	
2				○	
3				○	
4				○	
5				○	
6				○	
7				○	
8				○	
9				○	
10				○	
11				○	
12				○	
13				○	
14				○	
15				○	
16				○	
17				○	
18				○	
19				○	
20				○	

MONTHLY BUDGET

VARIABLE EXPENSES

#	DESCRIPTION	DATE	AMOUNT	PAID	COMMENT
21				○	
22				○	
23				○	
24				○	
25				○	
26				○	
27				○	
28				○	
29				○	
30				○	
31				○	
32				○	
33				○	
34				○	
35				○	
36				○	
37				○	
38				○	
39				○	
40				○	
41				○	
42				○	

MONTHLY SUMMARY

	BUDGETED	ACTUAL	DIFFERENCE
TOTAL INCOME			
TOTAL FIXED EXPENSES			
TOTAL VARIABLE EXPENSES			

DEBT REPAYMENT

DATE	ACCOUNT	STARTING BALANCE	MINIMUM PAYMENT	ADDITIONAL PAYMENT	BALANCE
TOTAL SPENT ON DEBTS THIS MONTH					

DAILY SPENDING TRACKER

JUNE 01	SPENT	JUNE 05	SPENT

JUNE 02	SPENT	JUNE 06	SPENT

JUNE 03	SPENT	JUNE 07	SPENT

JUNE 04	SPENT	JUNE 08	SPENT

DAILY SPENDING TRACKER

JUNE 09	SPENT	JUNE 13	SPENT

JUNE 10	SPENT	JUNE 14	SPENT

JUNE 11	SPENT	JUNE 15	SPENT

JUNE 12	SPENT	JUNE 16	SPENT

DAILY SPENDING TRACKER

JUNE 17	SPENT	JUNE 21	SPENT

JUNE 18	SPENT	JUNE 22	SPENT

JUNE 19	SPENT	JUNE 23	SPENT

JUNE 20	SPENT	JUNE 24	SPENT

DAILY SPENDING TRACKER

JUNE 25	SPENT	JUNE 29	SPENT

JUNE 26	SPENT	JUNE 30	SPENT

JUNE 27	SPENT

JUNE 28	SPENT

| TOTAL DAILY SPEND THIS MONTH | |

NOTES

_____
_____
_____
_____
_____
_____
_____
_____
_____
_____
_____
_____
_____
_____
_____
_____
_____
_____
_____
_____
_____
_____
_____

WHERE DID I HAVE THE MOST DIFFICULTY	HOW CAN I IMPROVE NEXT MONTH

JULY

NOTES	SUNDAY	MONDAY	TUESDAY
	3	4	5
	10	11	12
	17	18	19
	24	25	26
	31		

GOALS

OVERVIEW

WEDNESDAY	THURSDAY	FRIDAY	SATURDAY
		1	2
6	7	8	9
13	14	15	16
20	21	22	23
27	28	29	30

Never spend your money before you have earned it.

- Thomas Jefferson

MONTHLY BUDGET

INCOME

DATE	SOURCE	AMOUNT
	TOTAL	

SAVINGS

BUDGETED	ACTUAL
DIFFERENCE	

FIXED EXPENSES

#	DESCRIPTION	DUE DATE	AMOUNT	PAID	COMMENT
1				○	
2				○	
3				○	
4				○	
5				○	
6				○	
7				○	
8				○	
9				○	
10				○	
11				○	
12				○	
13				○	
14				○	
15				○	
16				○	
17				○	
18				○	
19				○	
20				○	

MONTHLY BUDGET

VARIABLE EXPENSES

#	DESCRIPTION	DATE	AMOUNT	PAID	COMMENT
21				◯	
22				◯	
23				◯	
24				◯	
25				◯	
26				◯	
27				◯	
28				◯	
29				◯	
30				◯	
31				◯	
32				◯	
33				◯	
34				◯	
35				◯	
36				◯	
37				◯	
38				◯	
39				◯	
40				◯	
41				◯	
42				◯	

MONTHLY SUMMARY

	BUDGETED	ACTUAL	DIFFERENCE
TOTAL INCOME			
TOTAL FIXED EXPENSES			
TOTAL VARIABLE EXPENSES			

DEBT REPAYMENT

DATE	ACCOUNT	STARTING BALANCE	MINIMUM PAYMENT	ADDITIONAL PAYMENT	BALANCE
	TOTAL SPENT ON DEBTS THIS MONTH				

DAILY SPENDING TRACKER

JULY 01	SPENT	JULY 05	SPENT

JULY 02	SPENT	JULY 06	SPENT

JULY 03	SPENT	JULY 07	SPENT

JULY 04	SPENT	JULY 08	SPENT

DAILY SPENDING TRACKER

JULY 09	SPENT	JULY 13	SPENT

JULY 10	SPENT	JULY 14	SPENT

JULY 11	SPENT	JULY 15	SPENT

JULY 12	SPENT	JULY 16	SPENT

DAILY SPENDING TRACKER

JULY 17	SPENT	JULY 21	SPENT

JULY 18	SPENT	JULY 22	SPENT

JULY 19	SPENT	JULY 23	SPENT

JULY 20	SPENT	JULY 24	SPENT

DAILY SPENDING TRACKER

JULY 25	SPENT	JULY 29	SPENT

JULY 26	SPENT	JULY 30	SPENT

JULY 27	SPENT	JULY 31	SPENT

JULY 28	SPENT		

TOTAL DAILY SPEND THIS MONTH	

NOTES

AUGUST

NOTES	SUNDAY	MONDAY	TUESDAY
_____ _____ _____ _____ _____ _____ _____ _____ _____ _____ _____ _____ _____ _____ _____ _____ _____ _____ _____ _____		1	2
	7	8	9
	14	15	16
	21	22	23
	28	29	30

GOALS

_____
_____
_____
_____

OVERVIEW

WEDNESDAY	THURSDAY	FRIDAY	SATURDAY
3	4	5	6
10	11	12	13
17	18	19	20
24	25	26	27
31			

AFFIRMATION:

Money flows to me from multiple sources.

MONTHLY BUDGET

INCOME

DATE	SOURCE	AMOUNT
	TOTAL	

SAVINGS

BUDGETED	ACTUAL
DIFFERENCE	

FIXED EXPENSES

#	DESCRIPTION	DUE DATE	AMOUNT	PAID	COMMENT
1				○	
2				○	
3				○	
4				○	
5				○	
6				○	
7				○	
8				○	
9				○	
10				○	
11				○	
12				○	
13				○	
14				○	
15				○	
16				○	
17				○	
18				○	
19				○	
20				○	

MONTHLY BUDGET

VARIABLE EXPENSES

#	DESCRIPTION	DATE	AMOUNT	PAID	COMMENT
21				◯	
22				◯	
23				◯	
24				◯	
25				◯	
26				◯	
27				◯	
28				◯	
29				◯	
30				◯	
31				◯	
32				◯	
33				◯	
34				◯	
35				◯	
36				◯	
37				◯	
38				◯	
39				◯	
40				◯	
41				◯	
42				◯	

MONTHLY SUMMARY

	BUDGETED	ACTUAL	DIFFERENCE
TOTAL INCOME			
TOTAL FIXED EXPENSES			
TOTAL VARIABLE EXPENSES			

DEBT REPAYMENT

DATE	ACCOUNT	STARTING BALANCE	MINIMUM PAYMENT	ADDITIONAL PAYMENT	BALANCE
TOTAL SPENT ON DEBTS THIS MONTH					

DAILY SPENDING TRACKER

AUGUST 01	SPENT

AUGUST 05	SPENT

AUGUST 02	SPENT

AUGUST 06	SPENT

AUGUST 03	SPENT

AUGUST 07	SPENT

AUGUST 04	SPENT

AUGUST 08	SPENT

DAILY SPENDING TRACKER

AUGUST 09	SPENT	AUGUST 13	SPENT

AUGUST 10	SPENT	AUGUST 14	SPENT

AUGUST 11	SPENT	AUGUST 15	SPENT

AUGUST 12	SPENT	AUGUST 16	SPENT

DAILY SPENDING TRACKER

AUGUST 17	SPENT	AUGUST 21	SPENT

AUGUST 18	SPENT	AUGUST 22	SPENT

AUGUST 19	SPENT	AUGUST 23	SPENT

AUGUST 20	SPENT	AUGUST 24	SPENT

DAILY SPENDING TRACKER

AUGUST 25	SPENT	AUGUST 29	SPENT

AUGUST 26	SPENT	AUGUST 30	SPENT

AUGUST 27	SPENT	AUGUST 31	SPENT

AUGUST 28	SPENT		
		TOTAL DAILY SPEND THIS MONTH	

NOTES

WHERE DID I HAVE THE MOST DIFFICULTY	HOW CAN I IMPROVE NEXT MONTH

SEPTEMBER

NOTES	SUNDAY	MONDAY	TUESDAY
_____			
_____	4	5	6
_____	11	12	13
_____	18	19	20
_____	25	26	27

GOALS

_____

_____

_____

_____

OVERVIEW

WEDNESDAY	THURSDAY	FRIDAY	SATURDAY
	1	2	3
7	8	9	10
14	15	16	17
21	22	23	24
28	29	30	

Wealth consists not in having great possessions,
but in having few wants.

- Epictetus

MONTHLY BUDGET

INCOME

DATE	SOURCE	AMOUNT
	TOTAL	

SAVINGS

BUDGETED	ACTUAL
DIFFERENCE	

FIXED EXPENSES

#	DESCRIPTION	DUE DATE	AMOUNT	PAID	COMMENT
1				◯	
2				◯	
3				◯	
4				◯	
5				◯	
6				◯	
7				◯	
8				◯	
9				◯	
10				◯	
11				◯	
12				◯	
13				◯	
14				◯	
15				◯	
16				◯	
17				◯	
18				◯	
19				◯	
20				◯	

MONTHLY BUDGET

VARIABLE EXPENSES

#	DESCRIPTION	DATE	AMOUNT	PAID	COMMENT
21				◯	
22				◯	
23				◯	
24				◯	
25				◯	
26				◯	
27				◯	
28				◯	
29				◯	
30				◯	
31				◯	
32				◯	
33				◯	
34				◯	
35				◯	
36				◯	
37				◯	
38				◯	
39				◯	
40				◯	
41				◯	
42				◯	

MONTHLY SUMMARY

	BUDGETED	ACTUAL	DIFFERENCE
TOTAL INCOME			
TOTAL FIXED EXPENSES			
TOTAL VARIABLE EXPENSES			

DEBT REPAYMENT

DATE	ACCOUNT	STARTING BALANCE	MINIMUM PAYMENT	ADDITIONAL PAYMENT	BALANCE
	TOTAL SPENT ON DEBTS THIS MONTH				

DAILY SPENDING TRACKER

SEPTEMBER 01	SPENT	SEPTEMBER 05	SPENT

SEPTEMBER 02	SPENT	SEPTEMBER 06	SPENT

SEPTEMBER 03	SPENT	SEPTEMBER 07	SPENT

SEPTEMBER 04	SPENT	SEPTEMBER 08	SPENT

DAILY SPENDING TRACKER

SEPTEMBER 09	SPENT	SEPTEMBER 13	SPENT

SEPTEMBER 10	SPENT	SEPTEMBER 14	SPENT

SEPTEMBER 11	SPENT	SEPTEMBER 15	SPENT

SEPTEMBER 12	SPENT	SEPTEMBER 16	SPENT

DAILY SPENDING TRACKER

SEPTEMBER 17	SPENT	SEPTEMBER 21	SPENT

SEPTEMBER 18	SPENT	SEPTEMBER 22	SPENT

SEPTEMBER 19	SPENT	SEPTEMBER 23	SPENT

SEPTEMBER 20	SPENT	SEPTEMBER 24	SPENT

DAILY SPENDING TRACKER

SEPTEMBER 25	SPENT	SEPTEMBER 29	SPENT

SEPTEMBER 26	SPENT	SEPTEMBER 30	SPENT

SEPTEMBER 27	SPENT		

SEPTEMBER 28	SPENT		
		TOTAL DAILY SPEND THIS MONTH	

NOTES

WHERE DID I HAVE THE MOST DIFFICULTY	HOW CAN I IMPROVE NEXT MONTH

OCTOBER

NOTES	SUNDAY	MONDAY	TUESDAY
	2	3	4
	9	10	11
	16	17	18
	23	24	25
	30	31	

GOALS

OVERVIEW

WEDNESDAY	THURSDAY	FRIDAY	SATURDAY
			1
5	6	7	8
12	13	14	15
19	20	21	22
26	27	28	29

A penny saved is a penny earned.

- Benjamin Franklin

MONTHLY BUDGET

INCOME

DATE	SOURCE	AMOUNT
	TOTAL	

SAVINGS

BUDGETED	ACTUAL
DIFFERENCE	

FIXED EXPENSES

#	DESCRIPTION	DUE DATE	AMOUNT	PAID	COMMENT
1				○	
2				○	
3				○	
4				○	
5				○	
6				○	
7				○	
8				○	
9				○	
10				○	
11				○	
12				○	
13				○	
14				○	
15				○	
16				○	
17				○	
18				○	
19				○	
20				○	

MONTHLY BUDGET

VARIABLE EXPENSES

#	DESCRIPTION	DATE	AMOUNT	PAID	COMMENT
21				○	
22				○	
23				○	
24				○	
25				○	
26				○	
27				○	
28				○	
29				○	
30				○	
31				○	
32				○	
33				○	
34				○	
35				○	
36				○	
37				○	
38				○	
39				○	
40				○	
41				○	
42				○	

MONTHLY SUMMARY

	BUDGETED	ACTUAL	DIFFERENCE
TOTAL INCOME			
TOTAL FIXED EXPENSES			
TOTAL VARIABLE EXPENSES			

DEBT REPAYMENT

DATE	ACCOUNT	STARTING BALANCE	MINIMUM PAYMENT	ADDITIONAL PAYMENT	BALANCE
TOTAL SPENT ON DEBTS THIS MONTH					

DAILY SPENDING TRACKER

OCTOBER 01	SPENT	OCTOBER 05	SPENT

OCTOBER 02	SPENT	OCTOBER 06	SPENT

OCTOBER 03	SPENT	OCTOBER 07	SPENT

OCTOBER 04	SPENT	OCTOBER 08	SPENT

DAILY SPENDING TRACKER

OCTOBER 09	SPENT	OCTOBER 13	SPENT

OCTOBER 10	SPENT	OCTOBER 14	SPENT

OCTOBER 11	SPENT	OCTOBER 15	SPENT

OCTOBER 12	SPENT	OCTOBER 16	SPENT

DAILY SPENDING TRACKER

OCTOBER 17	SPENT	OCTOBER 21	SPENT

OCTOBER 18	SPENT	OCTOBER 22	SPENT

OCTOBER 19	SPENT	OCTOBER 23	SPENT

OCTOBER 20	SPENT	OCTOBER 24	SPENT

DAILY SPENDING TRACKER

OCTOBER 25	SPENT	OCTOBER 29	SPENT

OCTOBER 26	SPENT	OCTOBER 30	SPENT

OCTOBER 27	SPENT	OCTOBER 31	SPENT

OCTOBER 28	SPENT		
		TOTAL DAILY SPEND THIS MONTH	

NOTES

_____

_____

_____

_____

_____

_____

_____

_____

_____

_____

_____

_____

_____

_____

_____

_____

_____

_____

_____

_____

_____

_____

_____

_____

WHERE DID I HAVE THE MOST DIFFICULTY	HOW CAN I IMPROVE NEXT MONTH

NOVEMBER

NOTES	SUNDAY	MONDAY	TUESDAY
			1
	6	7	8
	13	14	15
	20	21	22
	27	28	29

GOALS

_____

_____

_____

_____

OVERVIEW

WEDNESDAY	THURSDAY	FRIDAY	SATURDAY
2	3	4	5
9	10	11	12
16	17	18	19
23	24	25	26
30			

Don't give up what you want most, for what you want now.

MONTHLY BUDGET

INCOME

DATE	SOURCE	AMOUNT
	TOTAL	

SAVINGS

BUDGETED	ACTUAL
DIFFERENCE	

FIXED EXPENSES

#	DESCRIPTION	DUE DATE	AMOUNT	PAID	COMMENT
1				○	
2				○	
3				○	
4				○	
5				○	
6				○	
7				○	
8				○	
9				○	
10				○	
11				○	
12				○	
13				○	
14				○	
15				○	
16				○	
17				○	
18				○	
19				○	
20				○	

MONTHLY BUDGET

VARIABLE EXPENSES

#	DESCRIPTION	DATE	AMOUNT	PAID	COMMENT
21				○	
22				○	
23				○	
24				○	
25				○	
26				○	
27				○	
28				○	
29				○	
30				○	
31				○	
32				○	
33				○	
34				○	
35				○	
36				○	
37				○	
38				○	
39				○	
40				○	
41				○	
42				○	

MONTHLY SUMMARY

	BUDGETED	ACTUAL	DIFFERENCE
TOTAL INCOME			
TOTAL FIXED EXPENSES			
TOTAL VARIABLE EXPENSES			

DEBT REPAYMENT

DATE	ACCOUNT	STARTING BALANCE	MINIMUM PAYMENT	ADDITIONAL PAYMENT	BALANCE
TOTAL SPENT ON DEBTS THIS MONTH					

DAILY SPENDING TRACKER

NOVEMBER 01	SPENT	NOVEMBER 05	SPENT

NOVEMBER 02	SPENT	NOVEMBER 06	SPENT

NOVEMBER 03	SPENT	NOVEMBER 07	SPENT

NOVEMBER 04	SPENT	NOVEMBER 08	SPENT

DAILY SPENDING TRACKER

NOVEMBER 09	SPENT	NOVEMBER 13	SPENT

NOVEMBER 10	SPENT	NOVEMBER 14	SPENT

NOVEMBER 11	SPENT	NOVEMBER 15	SPENT

NOVEMBER 12	SPENT	NOVEMBER 16	SPENT

DAILY SPENDING TRACKER

NOVEMBER 17	SPENT	NOVEMBER 21	SPENT

NOVEMBER 18	SPENT	NOVEMBER 22	SPENT

NOVEMBER 19	SPENT	NOVEMBER 23	SPENT

NOVEMBER 20	SPENT	NOVEMBER 24	SPENT

DAILY SPENDING TRACKER

NOVEMBER 25	SPENT	NOVEMBER 29	SPENT

NOVEMBER 26	SPENT	NOVEMBER 30	SPENT

NOVEMBER 27	SPENT		

NOVEMBER 28	SPENT		
		TOTAL DAILY SPEND THIS MONTH	

NOTES

WHERE DID I HAVE THE MOST DIFFICULTY	HOW CAN I IMPROVE NEXT MONTH

DECEMBER

NOTES	SUNDAY	MONDAY	TUESDAY
_____ _____ _____ _____ _____ _____ _____			
_____ _____ _____ _____ _____ _____	4	5	6
_____ _____ _____ _____	11	12	13
_____ _____ _____ _____	18	19	20
_____ _____ _____ _____ _____	25	26	27

GOALS

_____

_____

_____

_____

OVERVIEW

WEDNESDAY	THURSDAY	FRIDAY	SATURDAY
	1	2	3
7	8	9	10
14	15	16	17
21	22	23	24
28	29	30	31

Beware of little expenses, a small leak will sink a great ship.

- Benjamin Franklin

MONTHLY BUDGET

INCOME

DATE	SOURCE	AMOUNT
	TOTAL	

SAVINGS

BUDGETED	ACTUAL
DIFFERENCE	

FIXED EXPENSES

#	DESCRIPTION	DUE DATE	AMOUNT	PAID	COMMENT
1				◯	
2				◯	
3				◯	
4				◯	
5				◯	
6				◯	
7				◯	
8				◯	
9				◯	
10				◯	
11				◯	
12				◯	
13				◯	
14				◯	
15				◯	
16				◯	
17				◯	
18				◯	
19				◯	
20				◯	

MONTHLY BUDGET

VARIABLE EXPENSES

#	DESCRIPTION	DATE	AMOUNT	PAID	COMMENT
21				○	
22				○	
23				○	
24				○	
25				○	
26				○	
27				○	
28				○	
29				○	
30				○	
31				○	
32				○	
33				○	
34				○	
35				○	
36				○	
37				○	
38				○	
39				○	
40				○	
41				○	
42				○	

MONTHLY SUMMARY

	BUDGETED	ACTUAL	DIFFERENCE
TOTAL INCOME			
TOTAL FIXED EXPENSES			
TOTAL VARIABLE EXPENSES			

DEBT REPAYMENT

DATE	ACCOUNT	STARTING BALANCE	MINIMUM PAYMENT	ADDITIONAL PAYMENT	BALANCE
TOTAL SPENT ON DEBTS THIS MONTH					

DAILY SPENDING TRACKER

DECEMBER 01	SPENT

DECEMBER 05	SPENT

DECEMBER 02	SPENT

DECEMBER 06	SPENT

DECEMBER 03	SPENT

DECEMBER 07	SPENT

DECEMBER 04	SPENT

DECEMBER 08	SPENT

DAILY SPENDING TRACKER

DECEMBER 09	SPENT	DECEMBER 13	SPENT

DECEMBER 10	SPENT	DECEMBER 14	SPENT

DECEMBER 11	SPENT	DECEMBER 15	SPENT

DECEMBER 12	SPENT	DECEMBER 16	SPENT

DAILY SPENDING TRACKER

DECEMBER 17	SPENT	DECEMBER 21	SPENT

DECEMBER 18	SPENT	DECEMBER 22	SPENT

DECEMBER 19	SPENT	DECEMBER 23	SPENT

DECEMBER 20	SPENT	DECEMBER 24	SPENT

DAILY SPENDING TRACKER

DECEMBER 25	SPENT	DECEMBER 29	SPENT

DECEMBER 26	SPENT	DECEMBER 30	SPENT

DECEMBER 27	SPENT	DECEMBER 31	SPENT

DECEMBER 28	SPENT		
		TOTAL DAILY SPEND THIS MONTH	

NOTES

WHERE DID I HAVE THE MOST DIFFICULTY	HOW CAN I IMPROVE NEXT MONTH

The goal isn't more money. The goal is living life on your own terms.

- Chris Brogan

YEAR END REVIEW

FINANCIAL SUMMARY

	TOTAL	COMMENTS
INCOME		
EXPENSES		
SAVINGS		
DEBT PAID		
ASSETS		
LIABILITIES		
NET WORTH		

WHERE DID I HAVE THE MOST DIFFICULTY THIS YEAR

_____

_____

_____

_____

_____

_____

HOW CAN I IMPROVE OR CHANGE MY APPROACH FOR NEXT YEAR

_____

_____

_____

_____

_____

_____

BIGGEST FINANCIAL ACCOMPLISHMENT THIS YEAR

_____

_____

_____

HOW WILL I REWARD MYSELF FOR THIS ACCOMPLISHMENT

_____

_____

_____

NOTES

NOTES

NOTES

NOTES

NOTES

TIME FOR A NEW PLANNER

I HOPE THIS SIMPLE BUDGET PLANNER HELPED YOU STAY ON TRACK
AND REACH YOUR FINANCIAL GOALS THIS YEAR.

IF YOU WOULD LIKE TO BE NOTIFIED WHEN THE NEW 2023 BUDGET PLANNERS
GO ON SALE, PLEASE CONSIDER FOLLOWING ME ON AMAZON.

WWW.AMAZON.COM/AUTHOR/EMMELINEBLOOM